The Answer to Each Is the Same

poetry
by

Pam O'Brien

2012

DOS MADRES PRESS INC.

P.O.Box 294, Loveland, Ohio 45140

www.dosmadres.com   editor@dosmadres.com

Dos Madres is dedicated to the belief that the small press is essential to the vitality of contemporary literature as a carrier of the new voice, as well as the older, sometimes forgotten voices of the past. And in an ever more virtual world, to the creation of fine books pleasing to the eye and hand.

Dos Madres is named in honor of Vera Murphy and Libbie Hughes, the "Dos Madres" whose contributions have made this press possible.

Dos Madres Press, Inc. is an Ohio Not For Profit Corporation and a 501 (c) (3) qualified public charity. Contributions are tax deductible.

Executive Editor: Robert J. Murphy

Illustration & Book Design: Elizabeth H. Murphy
www.illusionstudios.net

Typset in Adobe Garamond Pro & Still Time
ISBN 978-1-933675-78-7
Library of Congress Control Number: 2012939133

First Edition

ACKNOWLEDGMENTS

The following poems previously appeared in the same or similar form in these publications:

"Holy Ground", *Comstock Review Awards Edition*
"Penelope's Web", *Fickle Muses*
"At the Jade Buddha Temple in Shanghai", *Exit 13*
"The Sisters' Stories", *The Comstock Review*
"Mary Magdalene", *The Penwood Review*
"On Maureen's Graduation from Gallaudet", *Small Brushes*
"On Cerulli's 'Making a Woman'", *Riverspeak*
"The Fall", *Windhover*
"Mrs. Darling Speaks", *Willow Review*
"Harmony", *Clark Street Review*
"The Boy I Said I Loved at Seventeen", *Memoir (and)*
"Lost Again", *Nostalgia*
"Sailing", *Eclectic Woman: Sweet Annie & Sweet Pea Review*
"Sight", *Riverspeak*
"Counting Coupons with the Italian Ladies", *Rattle*
"The Prodigal Son's Mother Waits on the Front Porch", *Sharing*
"Three Strange Angels", *Exit 13*
"Coming Home", *Comstock Review Awards Edition*
"Red", *Spire Bonus Edition*
"Daphne and Apollo", *Ship of Fools*
"Morning Walk", *Always Looking*
"The Little Mermaid", *Hidden Oak*
"The Mama Dream", *Pittsburgh City Paper*
"Getting Grandma to Heaven Was Putting Grandpa through Hell", *Along the Lake, an Anthology*
"Susann", *Riverspeak*
"Not Seeing the Prado", *The Aurorean*
"Green", *Paper Street Press*
"Reunion of Echo and Narcissus", *The Comstock Review*

The author thanks two workshops, Salisbury Hill Poets and the Squirrel Hill Poetry Workshop, for their advice and support over many years.

CHAPBOOKS

Kaleidoscopes, Main Street Rag, 1999
Paper Dancing, Foothills Publishing, 2004
Acceptable Losses, Pudding House, 2010

for Juan DeOnate
with love and thanks

TABLE OF CONTENTS

What is worth living for?

And what is worth dying for?

There are only four questions of value in life, Don Octavio.
What is sacred?
Of what is spirit made?
What is worth living for,
and what is worth dying for?
The answer to each is the same: only love.

Don Juan, Don Juan Demarco

*W*hat is sacred?

Holy Ground

There are white caps
on the Sea of Galilee this morning,
and I am leaving you here on holy ground.
We have
     moved to the rhythm of the Scriptures
     danced with David before the Lord
     heard the tambourine beating like a heart
     tasted bread and wine in each new sunrise.

In this time of two together
I have melted into your presence
as you carried me on wind and waves
     pulled me up the dizzy blue of Mount Tabor.
There are white caps
on the Sea of Galilee this morning
and I am already thinking of missing you

wondering if I will sleep at night
without your whisper soft against my cheek
wondering if I will feel awake
without your hand leading me
round my dark, dark corners
into the light.

Penelope's Web

Still in the cashmere life, Penelope hides behind a veil.
Ulysses asks the king, *will you give me your daughter for my wife?*
She starts her weaving with Ulysses' eyelashes
making shadows on his cheeks.
She goes with him. Then she stays.

She stays behind when less than a year later
he leaves for the Trojan War, risk, years.
She stays and weaves eyelashes, the summer Sunday
they are in the sea wearing nothing but water,
the heat where his body stops, hers begins,
his voice dropping gentle at night,
his dark hand on her spine. She weaves from memory.

Her memories are a spider web around her heart.
She cannot break free. Each year when snow is melting
and green is shining through, new suitors beg her
to remarry, to forget the man who must surely be dead.
Penelope knows she will be trapped in now or trapped in then,
knows that her weaving keeps Ulysses alive,
alive enough so that when she reaches for him
on rainy March evenings, he is tucked away complete,
not one part of him lost.

She almost loses everything, for she promises
to take a new lover when her weaving is complete.
But she outwits them all, by night unravels
every stitch of her web, as if to say
this is enough, this waiting,
this doing and redoing,
this mystery,
this taking shape and growing,
this coming apart.

Listing

People say anxiety comes
when you think about
what might happen
when you lose the now.
The air thickens, the light dims.

I am anxious this morning.
outside the moment
chained to my to-do list
    call the dentist
    take Uncle Herbie to lunch
    weed the garden.

I should write on my list
    sit by the pond
    listen to the mourning dove in the hemlock
    eat Swiss cheese and think about each hole
    think a minute about each bite
    read "Querencia" by Stephen Dobyns
    say out loud *my husband has cancer.*

Grace

Nana Schmitt feared my father
would be her only child. Grampa held her close at night
said *God will provide a new baby.*
They just needed to trust, to wait.
Nana was bad at both.

One snowy Buffalo Saturday
she nudged Grampa awake
said *pack up Jackie, we're going
to the orphanage on Maple Drive.*
The old Buick stumbled its way across town.

Wandering the halls of the orphanage,
little Jackie whining because lunch was late,
Nana grew confused.
I guess I was wrong she said.
Today's not the day.

Spring was dancing its way alive
when Nana dragged Grampa
back for a second visit.
This time she knew right where to go,
which crib to head for,
which baby girl would nestle
into Grampa's chest
like it was the warm nest
she'd been hunting all week.

We're naming her Grace,
Nana told Grampa. *Hold her.*
This is what Grace feels like.

At the Jade Buddha Temple in Shanghai

Red silk streamers billow from trees,
carry the wishes of the faithful.
Incense burns in the courtyard braziers.
Monks wander the serpentine corridors.
Each room holds Buddha in a different form
with 24 arms, as a girl reclining,
a warrior surrounded by warriors.

I buy an extra 10 yuan ticket
to see the gleaming jade Buddha
to watch the pregnant women all in white
pay to have oil poured over his jade head
pay to receive the blessing.

They must be praying for sons.

As I prayed for you, Michael,
for the birth of my son.
And as I later prayed for
a way back into your heart,
a way to understand.

I stand on the second floor balcony
look down on the faithful
waving torches of incense
wonder if I should write your name
in gold on a red streamer
then pray to hear you through your silence
set you free on the wind in the branches.

The Sisters' Stories

When I go to Helen's house high in the Smoky Mountains,
she wants me with her in the calico bedroom
as she drags out the boxes, makes the myths alive again.

This is Sister Aggie's engagement picture.
She died two months before the wedding.
Acute indigestion, the obituary said. Sister Thelma
said it was poisoning. Such an imagination.
Here's Thelma when she graduated
from college. Only seventeen years old.
So smart. Always the smartest one.
That's my mother. My only picture of her.
She died when I was seven. I remember nothing of her.
I wonder, even now, sixty years later,
if it would hurt too much to remember.

Helen's eyes mirror the haze on the mountains
behind her, just before the afternoon shower.
My vision clouds over, too.
I travel her journey, stopping where she stops.

One day when mother was sick she tied me
to the bedpost so I wouldn't get hurt or lost.
She brushed and braided my hair.
Sometimes it grew wet with her tears.
Sometimes she cried all day.
That's my father with her. He left me
with the sisters after she died. Moved to Texas.
A railroad engineer. His new wife didn't want
him to visit me. I only have the sisters' stories.

We perch on the quilt high in the Smokies.
We go back for as long as she needs to be there.
If she could, she would say *Rumplestiltskin* aloud
and tell that story, too,
knowing somewhere inside her
that in the speaking, the naming,
there is power to go on.

Mary Magdalene

Perhaps Jesus cast seven demons from her.
She may be the prostitute of Luke's gospel
or the one who sold all she had
to dump expensive perfume on his feet, then wipe
the feet with her hair, her tears.

Is she the example of why Jesus did what he did,
the one who makes the cross make sense?
Probably she too spent time in a garden
with gnarled trees, waiting for soldiers,
listening to the snoring of sleeping friends
who promised to stand by her, stay awake.

Her shining moment is the Sunday
after not so good Friday.
At the empty tomb, she talks to angels.
Doesn't recognize them.
And she cries. Others go running off to tell others,

but Mary Magdalene, she stays there
maybe remembering the perfume and dirty feet
or the times she too felt betrayed and cried.
Maybe her own tears blind her
for when a man stops by, she thinks it's the gardener.
Until he says her name.
"Mary," he says.
It's Sunday dawn and there she is, the first person
to hear that voice alive again. Mary Magdalene,
that maybe whore,
that maybe perfume waster,
that first person to follow him on into Easter.

Wish List

I saw the rust-colored velvet dress one October morning
in the window of the town's department store.
It was short, sexy, soft. $35. Our rent was $65.
I hadn't had a new dress since the baby came.

It took me months of dragging
wet clothes home from the laundromat,
hanging them from curtain rods, door frames,
weeks of turning off lights,
turning down heat.
hoarding quarters, dollar bills
in Nana Ford's cracked tea pot
on the top shelf where
my husband wouldn't look.

That dress hung in my closet for years
long after I couldn't fit into a size 5,
long after the closet was jammed
with beautiful long broomstick skirts,
silky cream blouses

Now it's time to give the dress away
let go of that autumn
the rusted leaves, the burning maples,
the husband leaving.
And yet the time I learned
to put my own name
on my wish list.

On Maureen's Graduation From Gallaudet*

Raise your arms,
Wiggle your hands.
That's applause.

Touch just below your lips,
Then move your hands outward.
That's thank you.

Two hands make a fist,
A slight shake to the right
Near your shoulder.
Congratulations.

We cannot say in words
The love you bring us.
But there are signs.

*Gallaudet, located in Washington, DC, is the National School for the Deaf.

Rosales Revisto

When I finally walked back through Rosales Park
back through time with you
I wasn't sure it was real
even as I was putting
one foot in front of the other.
Hard to be there again
those many years later,
hard to breathe,
hard to listen with those older ears,
hard to hear of your losses, your changes,
hard to tell you of mine.
Even though we know
good places now,
hard to hold,
to touch again who we were.

Hard to believe I only cried once.

The College Graduate

When you breeze through the back door on Saturday
it will be to fill your car with what is yours.
We are a rest stop on your way to the future.

I wish I hadn't promised
to sort the attic, pack your treasures
into these old B.F. Fields boxes.

I save, I hold tight
the ugly china dog from the county fair,
your diorama of the Battle of Gettysburg.
I toss aside
a lone jack without the small rubber ball,
a knitting needle with no yarn,
an envelope, the letter long ago discarded,
your size-two hand-me-down sleeper,
too worn to be saved.

What We Keep

In my grandmother's kitchen I created art,
well, paint-by-numbers pictures
once a horse, once an Indian chief.
Nana talked non-stop as she lumbered
from fridge to stove to counter
an apron around her size 24 housedress.
I didn't listen very well,
my painting consuming me
my legs dangling from the chipped blue chair
my arms stretching across the white table
to reach my paints.

I don't remember what Nana was cooking
probably a pot roast
or what she told me
probably a story about
her trip to where Anne of Green Gables lived.
How we'd go there together some day.

But I still see those mornings
the tiny maple table lamp
lighting my painting
the sun through the window
making my grandmother shine.

In Praise of My Grandmother's List

Family comes first.
Always. No matter what.

Everything tastes better if you add
bacon or Swiss cheese.

Clean even where
it doesn't show.

You can turn any event into a celebration
with candles and white linen.

Keep track of baseball stats.
It keeps your mind sharp.

Don't throw clothes away.
Mend them. Especially socks.

Even in a good marriage,
you'll fight about money and children.

Good listeners are more popular
than good talkers.

It's okay to lie if it's to say
something nice about someone.

Moisturize your neck or you'll look
like a chicken when you're old.

Daughter

I wish my mother had told me
being her daughter wasn't going
to go all that well.
She was going to matter way too much
and I was going to end up
carrying her long past the heart attack,
the refusal of dialysis.

Even past the funeral
I'd be carrying her
into all those places she avoided
like the proverbial plague–
airports, libraries, oceans.
I expect I will never
leave her behind.

She is in my vegetable soup recipe,
the way I fold clothes.
Her dark hooded eyes stare
from the wedding picture in the guest room,
sultry, beautiful
not smiling, not even then.

She called her mother every morning
at 9 am. I should have called her more.

I envision my own daughter
in her grown up LA life
sitting in the soft afternoon
sipping wine amid bougainvillea
in a garden café. She smiles
and confides to her friend,
You know, I love her so much
but in some ways she's ruined my life.

On Cerulli's "Making a Woman"

I

Mother permed my hair last week
and now I smell like the pink Toni box.
I hate it, how each night
she winds the strands hard and nails each
with a bobby pin. I especially hate
the five bobby pins without rubber tips.
I hope she won't use those on the sides.
I hope I will be able to fall asleep.
Each morning she unwinds curls,
brushes too hard against my sore scalp,
smiles, says *you look so pretty.*
I wonder if I look even prettier in the pointy black shoes
I squeeze on for my first day of second grade.

II

Beth's Beauty Salon.
My daughter perches in the jacked up chair
while Beth perms Molly's hair.
Molly says this is longer
than she's ever waited for anything.
Finally the neutralizer. Then the rinse.
I take pictures of Molly in the blue plastic cape.
Beth and I ooh and aaah over curls
tumbling Molly's pale face.
Before I can stop myself, the words fall out.
You look so pretty.

Intermezzo for Isaac

Isaac, when you were a young boy,
God told your father to sacrifice you
on Mount Moriah. What did you feel
when you saw that knife over you?
What tune played through your head
for years after that?

Isaac, when you were a blind old man,
passing on the blessing to one
of the twin boys, wanting to bless
your favorite, Esau, the older,
there stood Jacob, God's favorite,
with food, with smells, with a touch like Esau.

Isaac, twice you were God's instrument
and God played you into strange melodies
where sometimes the only counterpoint
was to tune up without being able
to see the score in front of you,
to give in to that deepest music
both times you couldn't sing

when you were roped to a slab,
when you were blind in a chair.

The Fall

She works hard now.
She weeds, plants, builds fires.
She carries heavy things, scrubs, cooks.
But sometimes at night there is time just to sit
a few minutes by the fire. She gathers
the boys close to her, tells them the story,

the story of what happened back when
it was brighter and easier, when there was nothing
heavy to carry. She tells them of the day in the garden
when the creature circled itself around the tree,
told her she could be like her father
if she would eat from the tree. She is forthright
when she tells the boys that yes she did eat
and yes their dad ate too. She tells her boys
their grandfather made them leave the garden,
but looking back on it, she can't blame him.

By this time the boys are sleeping softly
in her lap. They've heard this story before.
She doesn't have a whole lot
of other stories to tell, time being still young.

She worries that the circling creature
may have meandered out of the garden,
may in fact be hiding in the corn field
or sunning by the river and she doesn't know
if her boys will recognize it and run away fast
like she tried to teach them.
She's not even sure if she would know it on sight.

Just that one creature, that one bite,
and there are gaps between her and her father,

gaps wide as the sky within herself.
She drifts off to sleep dreaming
about spaces
where there weren't spaces,
spaces that may never fill.

Of what is spirit made?

Mrs. Darling Speaks

What can you expect from a boy
whose address is second star to the
right and straight on till morning,
from a leader whose lost boy band is so divided
that each has his own hollowed out tree.

Be ready, my daughter,
when such a boy comes to your bedroom
seeking his shadow self.
Be watchful, my daughter.
Don't get stuck cleaning the hideout,
sewing on pockets,
measuring medicine onto tiny spoons.
Don't be the one who has to walk the plank.

Yet don't miss out on
an adventure with such a boy.
Practice telling good stories.
Leave your window open.
Learn to fly.

Harmony

I am like the last player
in Haydn's "Farewell Symphony."
This past year, my grandmother died,
then my mother. I sold our house,
left my job, moved 100 miles away.
The youngest child left for college,
500 miles away. All away.
So many players left the stage,
one by one. What was once so full,
so melodic, is much too still.
I'm the last one left playing,
wandering these different days.

But those are the days.
Each evening you come home
to this new home.
You and I alone again
after all these years.
We play Scrabble, talk politics,
explore our new city.
We practice our new parts.
I'm learning what I can afford to lose.
You're not on the list.
I sense your counter-melody
playing in the wings where
you spend your new days,
adding bass notes to my single symphony.

And I keep on playing
for you, my love,
because somewhere I suppose I know
that you would care the most if I didn't
and that ultimately what's lost in the leaving
is nothing against what's found.

The Boy I Said I Loved at Seventeen,

was full of angles, brittle places
probably broken off
by his father who drank too much
by his mother who worked too hard
at the printing shop and then at home
trying to keep that drifting family together.
The boy worked weekends
at the Powell Avenue gas station
saved his money for the 14-karat necklace
that he pushed into my hand on Christmas Eve.

I didn't have many nice things
one twin sweater set in a soft green
a tweed skirt.
I wore his necklace with that.
I lost his gift.
On the bus to school, it circled my neck.
By lunch, gone.

I didn't want to tell him. He noticed right away,
yelled about how many Sundays
of pumping gas that gold chain cost.

Later I left Erie,
enlisted as the scholarship girl at a ritzy college.
He joined the Navy.
We stayed in touch, but you know the old story,
it was never the same.

It was about something
we couldn't name at seventeen.
and barely know it now.

The Day She Said Goodbye

Today she bounced up behind me
captured me in a hug
stepped back.

Don't turn around, Mom.
Listen.
Don't look.
This is hard to say.
Remember I liked Jimmy Swanson?
Well, I don't anymore.
And now I like Vince Agresti.
He's real short.
Don't look at me.
I'm meeting him
at the school picnic tomorrow
at the roller coaster
at two o'clock.

Before I could turn,
she had flown,
past the fingertips
of my outstretched hand.

Spinning the Body Pass

Back in the bad-first-marriage days
of the husband who didn't
want a pregnant wife or a baby,
of the in-laws who felt sorry for *their* baby boy,
I was trying damn hard
working days at the hospital
modeling weekends at the department store
starting a little girls' majorette group.

One thing I wasn't doing that Spring
was telling the husband to quit writing
unproducible plays and consider a day job.
Mostly what I wasn't doing was leaving.

Friday nights I wheeled the baby to the Y.
For 90 minutes I taught fifteen
grade-school girls with batons–
three Angelas, I think–
to twirl the figure eight, spin the body pass.
With the moms I sewed
black leotards, bow ties, top hats
and those Top Hats marched in area parades,
even won a few firsts.

That July, I invited the in-laws and the laws
to a summer picnic, made fried chicken and potato salad,
wanted them to *ooh* and *aah* over the baby,
watch the Top Hats win another prize,
wanted family to help me
make us look like
we were coming together
doing just fine.

It would be years before
I would take the baby and leave,
more years before I would finally give
up on making a family
out of people
who weren't.

David Is Back on DVD

I thought I left David behind me forever
when we divorced. Goodbye.
Good riddance. All that.

Oh sure, we pass each other at graduations, weddings.
Once David called to ask me to help his mother.
He lived 3,000 miles away.
I was five minutes from her.
I smuggled cigarettes into her
assisted living village, drove her
to the hospital to visit her husband
dying from smoking.

But it's not over. David is back
because of the granddaughter we share.
David is back on the DVDs
our son sends. David rocks Maggie.
David sits at the Thanksgiving table
in the chair I'll be in for Christmas.
Maggie chases his dog around the living room.
His wife mashes the potatoes.

David is wealthy now, has a dog,
a wife who stays.
I hate it that we are still family
even as I realize that it's not just him
but my aversion to the woman I was.

Yet how I love our son,
our son we created,
our son who edits, splices,
writes new scripts to create his dream,
this video scrapbook family.

Lost Again

Today I saw Robbie in the parking lot,
arms loaded with books,
a toddler tugging at his coat.
He slammed his car door shut
the way he used to shut his locker
back when we were sixteen.

Just that, and I am sixteen again.

Summer is over.
The nights are turning navy blue.
The September wind is panting over the lake,
whipping up curls and spray.

Just Robbie slamming a door shut
opens doors for me.
And I am lost again
in the taste of cider,
the smell of rain on wet leaf sidewalks,
the sound of mallards calling across the bay,
the look of boats out of their wet kingdoms
raised on winter wooden thrones,
the touch of his hand
when he tipped my face toward his.

Sailing

The summer we crewed together
the water was a color I haven't seen since.
My heart flaps in the wind,
straining to touch that time once more,
moving to memory.
I know I'm trawling the past,
body snatching in broad daylight.

We chance meet at the library.
I smile down at the sturdy son hugging your knees.
You examine my book, ask what courses I'm teaching.
I can't even remember.

I don't tell you that sometimes I still dream
I'm holding the child we never had.
I don't tell you
I've stopped calling you "my old lover,"
christened you "my old friend."

It's bad luck to rename a boat.

How to Say Goodbye to Your Mother

It starts in summer when she misses big family events.
She says bronchitis. Pneumonia. But you know she hates
large groups, fuss. She's adept at ducking places where she
feels shy, especially since daddy died. You'd think after ten
years she could find her way alone. But no. She lives with
your sister. Doesn't drive. Says she's too old to learn. She's
sixty-nine. By fall, the doctors say congestive heart failure.
You take her shopping. She's winded halfway through the
produce aisle. You know she still sneaks cigarettes. You
say nothing. She's hospitalized in January, rejects surgery.
When her kidneys start to fail in February, she rejects
dialysis. That last March week, you're so furious with your
mother you can barely speak when you enter the hospital's
step-down unit each morning. What about her grandson's
graduation? What about the family wedding? She asks you
to shampoo her hair. Hold her hand. Rub her feet. She tells
you she knows she's dying. You say she could still choose.
Surgery. Dialysis. Life. She ignores you. You sleep on the
couch in her room. The nurse wakes you to say this might
be your mother's last breath. You tell her you love her, miss
her already. You hold her through her last big event.

Still So Many Days I Want Her Back

I want to see her fertilize her Jackson Perkins roses,
help her play solitaire
while listening to the Cleveland Indians on the radio.
I want her to tell me why
my German potato salad doesn't taste like hers.
I want her to hem my dresses and make my marble birthday cake.

I want to hear her words again.

At my first wedding, she told me
there would only be room
for one shining star in the relationship
and it wouldn't be me.
I should have listened.

When she was 90,
she told me she liked it because
there wasn't as much peer pressure.

When I was in college, I told her
Aunt Sally seemed sad,
I whispered, *Nana, I think
something's happened to her.*
She put her arm around me, whispered back,
Honey, something happens to everyone.

Sight

In third grade I couldn't read
the board any more. I thought
Mrs. Murtland didn't press down
very hard with the chalk
like Mrs. Skinner did in second grade.
I stayed in at recess and copied down
vocabulary words and multiplication problems.
Months later, they had me read a chart
in the nurse's office. I couldn't.
My father drove me to a doctor
who put stinging drops in my eyes.
It was like crying.
I sat in the dark so long,
I thought I had missed dinner.
I misread more charts.

The next week my father left work early again.
He reminded me that he had left early twice.
We picked up my thick, black glasses.
I saw myself in the mirror and didn't cry
until later, in the bathroom.
We went out into the fading day
and I could read the storefront signs.
Hair by Joyce. Gustafson Optical.
I saw things differently,
became my own worst watcher.

Counting Coupons with the Italian Ladies

My mother marched across the street, convinced
Al Vicks to give me a job,
anything at all would be fine,
as long as it kept me off the beach,
as long as my 15-year-old body
in the pink bikini wasn't beckoning
to every boy who passed by.

The next Monday, there I was
the youngest girl at PA Food Merchants Assn.
eight to five
third floor
screeching window fans
counting coupons with six loud ladies
sliding those coupons into wooden slots
Palmolive on the far left
Colgate in the middle
Campbells on the right
ranking them
5
10
15
cents.

There I was
the only worker under 50,
the only one who didn't speak Italian.
The ladies bellowed *scusa, aiutare, cuore, luce.*
Sometimes they fed me bites
of their lunches, leftover casseroles,
garlic, flat noodles.

Angie, Lena, Marion, Maria
and two others whose names are gone now.
They talked about grandchildren, bunions,
red peppers on sale at the A&P,
stroked my hair, called me *bella,*
things my mother never did.

The Stolen Child

For he comes, the human child,
to the woods and waters wild,
with a fairy hand in hand.
For the world's more full of weeping
than he can understand.

W. B. Yeats

Years ago I blamed my mother for everything.
Queen of guilt, manipulation, cold.
Now I see differently, how ill-suited
for each other we were, how crazy
I must have made her with my wildness,
how crazy she made me with her control.

This year, I wonder about you, my son,
whether you still see us as ill-suited, why you don't cry,
what story stays hidden, what silence holds.
In five months when you become a father
I wonder how you will break open.

Your child will change you, Michael.
You will take parts you used to lock away
gently into your hands, hold them tight.
You will rock those lonely spaces, sing to them.
Trust me when I tell you they will love the music.
Yes, if you open Pandora's box
evil things will fly about. But after that,
at the bottom, you'll find hope.
Perhaps then you'll tell me what I'm leaving out.

The Prodigal Son's Mother Waits on the Front Porch

For Rika

I wonder about the mother
while the Prodigal Son is in the Far Country
squandering the inheritance
and later eating what the pigs didn't touch.

I propose that for the mother,
pacing the front porch,
this time is harder that the before or after.
This is waiting time,
trusting no one but God time,
I'm-not-sure-I'll-ever-see-my-boy-again time.

For each of us who have spent time
in the emergency room,
in the principal's office,
in the three a.m. looking-out-the-window time,
we know. We know
about the amusement park fun house
where suddenly we are too far in to get out,
where floors slip away, doors aren't there,
lights flicker, dim, go black.
Screams are heard.
Sometimes they are ours.
On the front porch, in our own Far Country,
we learn the language
of despair,
of waiting,
and if we know God,
of hope.

Signs

Our car knows the routine,
heads straight for the *Departing Flights* lane.
Two days before Christmas so
the plane is overbooked of course.
I sit near gate 51 next to
three businessmen from Boise
stranded since their Denver plane
sits snowed in at O'Hare.
Their gate blinks *Denver 2605*
cancelled. Still they sit.
My gate flashes
Los Angeles 1480 on time.

We're on our way to a California Christmas
my daughter's first in her own home
as a married woman.
Our home empty this year except for
our little Sheltie and dog sitter visits.
Our Pittsburgh cottage not the center
of turkey, presents, candles, board games.

Yet I'm eager to see what she'll do.
How will Christmas be different?
Will she carry on our traditions?
Just be supportive
I whisper to myself.
Just offer praise.
Don't try to take over.
Listen. Smile.

Heading down the LAX hall I spot
the arrow overhead that points the way.
Baggage claim. How appropriate.

Big Holidays

We did the holidays big.
Grandparents, aunts, uncles, cousins
jammed into one candle-rich dining room
passing gravy boats and olive trays
speculating on whether the cows
on Uncle Donny's farm would make it through the blizzard
whether Uncle Jerry would leave that damned Rockette
and come back to Aunt Grace.

Usually around coffee and pie time
Stan would move us all to remember
when he first saw Nana in the club in Schenectady
when he bought the neon sign business
even though Nana said he'd lose his shirt
and now he drives a Lincoln.

I was six, eight, ten then.
Stan hadn't had his first, second, third heart attack.

I remember my mother, dark circles under her eyes
running from kitchen to table
smiling at Stan's jokes
refilling Uncle Herbie's highball glass,
my Shirley Temple.
Keeping us all going.

I put in my years of doing holidays big.
Silver, china, hors d'oeuvres, starched napkins
then collapsing the next day.
That's how we did it.

This year my newlywed daughter hosted her first holiday dinner.
Only six of us. Turkey in a deep fryer,
everyday dishes, Mickey Mouse flatware.
But we sat around that table for hours laughing
then headed off to the living room to play Trivial Pursuit.

Gretel/Hansel

For John

Poor sister and brother. Poor children
of a woodcutter and a wicked second wife
who ditch children in the forest.

Poor children who stumble
on the sweetest little house
where, you know the story,
they gorge on sections of roof
until the old lady invites them in,
makes them pancakes for dinner, pours hot chocolate.
Little do those poor children know
she wants red meat, plans to eat
Hansel once she fattens him up.
Little does the old witch know
Gretel is planning to bake
the ancient biddy in the oven
instead of the daily bread.

Once the witch is toast,
Hansel and Gretel fill their pockets
with sweets and pearls and precious stones,
wander home to a long dead stepmother,
a deadbeat dad.

In this poor tale, the Grimms abandon *happily ever after.*
They know adults aren't all that dependable
know Gretel will be muttering
all through her twenties, into her thirties
how only your other half
can save you from witches and forests,
how only your brother will leave you
that trail of pebbles
shining like stars.

Dear S.W.,

Thanks for the postcard. Glad you like palace life.

Lots of nights, I think back to when you lived in our cottage.
You swept our floors, emptied our ashtrays,
made that chicken stew with moist dumplings
floating on top.
I remember how you told us
the plot to *Roman Holiday* and sang *Moon River* at night.

Two of my brothers thought bad luck would follow you always.
You know, poisoned combs, bad apples.
But I knew you would be o.k., dear S.W.,
even when I saw you in that glass coffin. And now, there you are
in a castle with a moat and all.

I know you told me any gnome girl would be proud to have me,
but after being your friend I wanted more.

Mostly, I wish I could have been a bigger man.

Affectionately,
B.

Three Strange Angels

What is the knocking
What is the knocking at the door at night?
It is somebody wants to do us harm.

No, no, it is the three strange angels.
Admit them, admit them.

            D. H. Lawrence

Three strange angels waited for me
on this return to Spain.
Rain. Space. And time.

Beach after beach
gray, sodden, toneless.
I saw the waves
back and forth back and forth
my head turning in time to the windshield wipers.

Spain seemed bigger too.
Not golden, intimate
but a place where I could get lost.
I would lose my direction on rotaries
veer off to a part of the pueblo
with no Roman bridge, no carved shimmering stone
find myself in the part with shabby bars
full of stale cheese bocadillos and flies.

Before, I was young, beautiful, busy–
Now, there was time to waste.
No rush to tan in the elusive sun.
No agenda to follow in each sodden, sandy town.
Long hours wandering puddled streets
wondering why wastebaskets and designer handbags
were sold in the same store.
Time to watch young mothers nudge their babies

awake, hum to them.
Time to feel my eyes mist over
as old men wheeled their hobbled wives
to stare in jewelry store windows.

*W*hat is worth living for?

Sketches of Spain

My husband wants to be a sculptor
quit his day job at the ad agency
buy a casita on the Mediterranean.
He's narrowed it down to Cabo de Gato
near the good alabaster.
He says we'll fly to Lucca occasionally
purchase slabs of marble
from the quarries used by Michaelangelo
tons of ghostly stone so heavy
we couldn't possibly
haul them home
but that husband, he knows a way.

Part of me is terrified
but another part is already packed.
At the casita I'll write extravagant poetry
and make gazpacho in tiny brown crocks
and hardly give a thought to
the kids in DC or my
teaching back in Pittsburgh.
No, I'll wander the streets of Nerja
learn if bougainvillea blooms
year round.

On our honeymoon that husband
tried to find us jobs at Disney World
so we wouldn't have to go home to the snow belt.
His dreams rearrange the way I think
almost convince me that living on the edge
doesn't necessarily mean I'll
fall off.

Thankful, Kind Of

I try to find a blessing in a husband
who has a heart attack one January
and cancer the next.
And he is still here so I do feel blessed.

Yes, briefly, candles in the bedroom,
late night whispered talk,
that desperate needing of each other.

When my son was born
I was amazed at the slippery wetness
of him sliding from my body,
his stare as I smiled above him,
the way he grabbed my finger.

Yet all those nights so desperate for sleep
wandering the narrow apartment hall
humming to him, patting him,
sometimes crying on his tiny bald head.

And the fear I would drop him
or forget him somewhere
or find some other way to ruin his life.

You know what I mean.
That kind of gratitude.
That kind of maybe thanks.

In Madrid

A blind crone squatted
on a green striped mat
near Moncloa subway station.
She sold apples
ten pesetas each
(but only five
at the vegetable stand next store).
I passed her each morning
on my way to the university.
Whenever generous relatives sent money
I bought her apples.
She learned my voice,
called me señorita Americana
told me I was beautiful.

I wondered if she pictured
her apples red or green,
if she felt her way home at night.
My nights belonged to a Spanish poet,
gleaming, dark, full of mystery words.
When I left Madrid, I thought
I was coming home to live
forever as the beautiful señorita americana
without the blind old woman
selling apples at Moncloa.

She lives with me still.
Like his eyes.

The Dance

The heat followed us as we left the subway
for Las Ventas. *Estudiantes,*
we could not afford the *sombra* tickets,
which would have gifted us with shade.
Instead we chose *sol,* heat, sun,
your hand pulling me to higher, hotter seats,
your voice like velvet on my cheek,
explaining the Spaniards' love of the music,
the dance between perfect poised matador,
wounded plodding bull. I, *la americana,*
was sorry for the bull, destined one way
or another to lose.

I read, years later in *El Sol*
of a matador gored by a bull in Malaga.
Both died, but that was
a rare instance, an exception,
that eventual surrender
to the heat
the difference
the dance.

Gracie's Elegy

Aunt Gracie was the family secret,
whispered about at the reunions
when those of the cousins who had
called her "aunt" and not "mother"
would huddle together, speculate on her death,
repeat the rumors, add to them.
Whether her life unraveled in a lost college love,
a wandering then lost husband
or years of found vodka,
we were happy to add more yarn to the skein,
to the tales we spun over the years.

Sometimes Grandfather would catch us at it,
scold us for speaking ill of the dead,
remind us Aunt Gracie died of pneumonia.
Would we please put more olives and some
of those sweet gherkin pickles on the relish tray?

And those of the cousins who called Aunt Gracie
mother and not aunt, had long before
been shipped off to foster homes,
or sent away to military school,
or run away, or simply disappeared.

It wasn't until years later
when Grandfather was doing his own dying
that those children of Gracie
came seeking their cousins.
We begged them for the true story,
the what-really-happened. They knew
less than we did, asked us why their
mother died. All that was left was
to welcome them back.
Family is family, as Grandfather would say.

We mentioned pneumonia, filled the relish tray
with olives and sweet gherkin pickles,
unraveled the threads
leading out of the labyrinth.

Coming Home

The finches found my feeder
this March morning.
Where have they been since October?
I can't believe each fall they know their route,
Mississauga, Tonawanda,
Savannah, Sarasota and then
know just what day
to head back north to me.
They arrive promptly
when I have seen the Spring sun,
felt greening warmth,
filled the feeder.
I can't believe it is planned.

I can't believe you came back on purpose
sensed that Spring had come again
took up your travel home
moved onto the familiar perch.

It must have been some chance.
Some crazy chance.

Red

Wolf: Where does she live?
Red Riding Hood: A good quarter of an hour farther into the wood.
Her house stands under three big oak trees,
near a hedge of nut trees which you must know.

                          The Brothers Grimm

That's right. Read the epigraph.
I gave that wolf clear directions to Granny's.
Honey, I'm no innocent.
I'm way past the Crayola stage.
Think about it.
What mama sends her kindergartener
into the woods alone?
What red hot female chooses
her grandmother over a wolf?

Sure, I had my red cape on,
along with my size four slinky sheath,
red stiletto heels.
Not hardly hiking-in-the-woods clothes.

And now, years later,
don't be thinking I'm sorry, honey.
The lovers who came after were nothing,
you hear me, nothing
to the feel of his hot pelt against my thighs,
the wet-fern smell of him,
his lips as he wolfed me down.

Daphne and Apollo

A typical story. He falls in love.
She runs away. He chases her.
She runs farther. And on and on.
He fails to detain her,
deter her, lure her from flight.
It is more than Apollo she is running from.
She's fleeing intimacy, civilization, the routine
of talk-to-me, let's-work-this-out.

And she does escape. Her father, the river god,
hears her prayer and changes Daphne,
a woman of the woods, into part
of the woods, a tree.
She gains the solitary,
freedom from the day-to-day
burdens of relationship.

How could she know that Apollo
would caress her barky skin, her leafy hair,
choose to weave his own crown of those leaves,
choose part of her to round
himself out, complete his image?

Looking back on it
rooted
green
immobile
she thinks attachment
may have been
the wiser choice.

For the Insomniacs

Insomniacs fit into small spaces,
dark corners, always aware
of their bodies as if they sense
sleep might force them
to wake as someone other
than themselves. I love
the way they grow
oh not comfortable but
familiar with night
     its windy fears
     its quiet creaks
     its dangerous clock curves.

My insomniac son-in-law
married a girl who can
fall asleep standing up
in the middle of conversation
in mid sentence even.
She tells me, "Mom, he doesn't
sleep well. He roams around."

Of course he does.
How could he not when at four
his mother left, when he could
never stop, not even with
three jobs, when he worked for eight
years to be the first from his family
to finish college. And now the PhD.
His life has no space for
lazy days, sleeping in.

How could he not when now
he must protect, provide for
his sleeping beauty, ever
vigilant for that moment
it is time to kiss her awake.

Say on guard, be alert, my son.
Weave your kingdom so tightly together
it can never unravel.

Full Circle

When I was six I rolled down
the hill behind our house over
and over until when I hit bottom
I looked up and the sky
would spin and spin.
It was all magic then. So was I.

Somehow I dropped pieces of that
hill-roller all over the place
for the next twenty years.
I lost pieces in the sunny, sweet, voracious children,
the career I chose so I would have "something to fall back on,"
the trying to please a man without magic.

But now. Now
I'm spinning, rolling again.
I'm picking up what simmers, shimmers.
I'm doing more of everything.
I'm floating wild in contradictions.
I'm swimming out over my head,
where magic can be found,
where I might drown.

Morning Walk

Most mornings after breakfast
I still pound the sidewalk.
Early sun,
my little Sheltie leads the way,
coffee steams in my thermal mug.
Today we take the service road
that winds along the light rail line.
Two miles in 40 minutes.

As I round the turn for home
I remind myself
to grab this dawn
to call this a moment to remember.
Nothing much is going on.
Everything is going on.
The wind washes my face clean. It's
like Vivaldi on a snowy day
like blueberries in cream
like holding my first granddaughter
when she was one hour old.

The Little Mermaid

My eyes extend beyond the farthest bloom of the waves;
I lose and find myself in the long water...
Theodore Roethke

On your sixteenth birthday
you swim to the surface for a day
and finally see the strange creatures
of your grandmother's stories.
The ones who walk.

And you want legs, too.
You want to live in the palace,
escape the danger of being submerged
or of drowning in that long water.
So you strike a deal with the sea witch.
She takes your voice and delivers the handsome prince.

And now you are like them,
except for the long silence
that follows you everywhere.

Prufrock claimed he heard the mermaids
singing each to each. But you,
now beyond that farthest bloom of the waves,
you must learn to sing to your prince
from the other side of words.

Witness

Sometimes I wonder why my life should be
this one, in this town, with this man.

Plumbers destroyed our front yard this March.
New sewer lines. Downed trees. Mountains of dirt.
Piled rocks. Crushed flagstone walk.

I'm forced to the back yard to discover
a hawk that screeches every seven seconds
baby cardinals practicing flight
over the cardinal flowers in the pond
wild ferns encroaching from the wood's edge

like your illness
consuming you, consuming us.
You keep me tight to my promise
to be a witness to your pain
the one who will remember
      key chains with duplicate keys
      wounds that reopen when touched
      hurts that need rubbing to heal.

And then, if you are gone, what will I do?

Draw myself a map to where I can still live.
Learn to fly in a softer space.

And what is worth dying for?

Juana la Zoca (Crazy Jane)

Did he die or did she die?
Seemed to die or died they both?…
Love is like the lion's tooth.
    "Crazy Jane Grown Old Looks at the Dancers"
                William Butler Yeats

Ferdinand and Isabella did more than outfit ships,
send Christopher Columbus on his way to discover
what he hoped was India or the new Jerusalem.
They shared a daughter, Jane, whose life
was more about not finding
a new way to anywhere at all.

The royal parents married her off
to the son of the Holy Roman Emperor.
One look at Philip the Beautiful
the drop-dead gorgeous German playboy
and Juana began her voyage to unhappiness.

He abandoned her in Spain. She refused
to eat or sleep until she trailed him back
to Germany. He caught fever and died.
She refused to have him buried,
stayed with him night and day.

Finally, they interred him
at Santa Clara Convent
and Jane buried herself in a room
with a window overlooking the graveyard.

She never left that room,
stayed 47 years, rocking,
watching the patch of ground that blanketed
her beautiful husband.

It was enough for her.
The Spaniards called her Juana la Loca.
Crazy Jane. Crazy, crazy Jane.

The Song of Simon's Wife

That first autumn afternoon,
that first time I saw him by the Sea of Galilee,
he was helping Andrew beach the boat,
one strong leg on the sand, one on the bow,
arms glistening as he hauled the fish nets ashore,
red hair glistening against the sun dipping red.
He married me one year later.
I knew so well this man who loved
to stand outside in thunderstorms,
knew the triangular scar on his thigh,
knew that the blue tunic I wove for him
made his eyes like the misty May sea.

He told me after he met the new rabbi
that one day this teacher would come
and he would go. Simon, my Simon,
leave me? Never, I thought.
But that Jesus returned and Simon did leave.

When Simon finally came home, he told me he had failed,
had denied Jesus three times. I held his blue tunic wet and close
as I washed it. I begged him to stay home,
but he left again, walking out into the sunset
on fire for this Jesus who was somehow still alive, who
was the lord of all life, especially my Simon's life.

One of Simon's friends wrote me
that Simon was crucified in Rome,
hung upside down, that in his last days
Simon was called Peter,
the rock that church of Jesus would rest on.
I pictured Simon wrapping that hope around
himself like his old blue tunic.

I don't want to remember him hanging
upside down in Rome.
So instead I relive the morning I lay
in the crook of his arm and traced
patterns on his chest with my finger.
I carried hot bread and oil to him at lunchtime, said
This is for you. Eat.

Other times I remember
Simon's story after he denied Jesus three times
and Jesus came back to life.
This raised up Jesus appeared
to my Simon three times, asked: *Simon, do you love me?*
And Simon said yes three times.

Somehow, by love and forgiveness,
Jesus moved Simon's denials
one
by
one
by
one
over to the positive side.
I count them, finger them still,
like colored beads on an abacus.

How He Provided

My father smoked, back when smoking
was manly, sociable, didn't cause cancer.
Every day he was the first to rise,
made my fried egg breakfast,
packed two bologna sandwiches for his lunch,
left 50 cents on the counter for my lunch,
stuffed a new pack of Marlboro's in his shirt pocket.
I would hear his ancient Chevy backing out
of the driveway, as the sun rose,
as I pulled pink foam curlers from my hair.

I never thought of him as I walked
through my days of classes, cafeteria,
smiles from boys, notes from girls.
I never saw him at his drafting table
that perfect printing on the blueprints
those endless cups of coffee
that ashtray filling up.

He would walk in the door at 5:30.
I never saw him tired
but he must have been.
He never stopped at a bar,
went out only to bowl or pick up groceries.

This is how he provided.
This is what he knew how to do.

Such a Difference between Quiet and Silence

Maggie, my tiny granddaughter,
awakens too early from her stroller nap
cries for at least ten minutes.
Later, we wolf down spaghetti at Maggione's.
Back home, I give
Maggie her bath, her bottle.
tiptoe out of her darkened room.
Take a few moments in the quiet.

I call my college friend Karin
who lost her only child
two years ago today.
Karin speaks at a church this week
tells her story of Kristina's suicide.
later meets Kristina's friends
for coffee, more remembering.
That night, in Kristina's old room,
Karin fingers the silence of
her daughter's last grocery list.

What She Couldn't Have Known

For Karin and Bill

what's left are the photos
on stands
in frames
in books
collages of her life fill the house

what's left are the words
her poems
her papers
her journals
even her address book
her last grocery list matters now

mostly though
what's left are the gaps
she couldn't have known how it would be
none of them who leave
when we're not done needing them know
she can't possibly have known
the empty spaces left
not just corners or closet shelves
but huge ballrooms, entire dining rooms
the deep holes we now have to keep
walking around
sometimes wishing we could fall in too

but we stay
circling the absence

this is what
she couldn't have known

The Mama Dream

It is always raining.
I am back in my mother's house,
now remodeled.
She is dying and we all know this.

Mama's bed is in the living room.
She shivers under her faded red quilt
and when there is a break in conversation
I tell her this is not something she would do in real life.

The rain outside floats inside.

Aunt Sally brings me chardonnay.
My sister disappears into the empty rooms.
Mama, whose house was her very existence,
doesn't care if her bed isn't where it belongs.

I take Mama to the wharf,
convince her to try the roof walk.
I wear my red slip, climb the narrow, crooked stairs,
joke with burly sailors.

At the top, we walk the tar roof,
watch the boats beyond.
I could stay there forever in rain and mist.

I wish I had asked Mama if she saw
distant boats flying jibs,
if she sensed the other women,
if we watched this
together or as one.

I wish I had I asked if I am sailing on alone.

Getting Grandma to Heaven
Was Putting Grandpa through Hell

At least that's what he told the neighbors
when they stopped by with still warm cookies,
little notes for him to take to Grandma
in the hospital. It was winter and they were afraid
to drive the fifteen miles themselves
what with the roads being icy, but they sent
their cards, their prayers.
Grandpa drove in every morning, stayed until dark,
fed her small scoops of french vanilla ice cream,
reminded her of the time he carried the white iced
wedding cake through downtown Buffalo in a snow storm,
and of the day Carol brought home straight "A"s
on her report card and Grace hid hers because
the only good thing was "excellent home economics skills"

One day Grandma told him she was dying.
He called the pastor who drove
the slipping roads with three key deacons.
They prayed, sang "Amazing Grace" and
shared communion with Grandma,
who closed her eyes, sank back,
grew smaller, stiller, softer.
Grandpa's tears ran onto his hand,
then onto hers held in his.
Ten minutes later Grandma opened her eyes,
said, *well, that didn't work*
and asked for a turkey sandwich.

Grandpa grew frail fighting the Buffalo snows
and trying to remember good stories to tell.
His mind fixed on the 1956 Thanksgiving
when she burned the turkey, on how before

this mad-cell-spread invaded her flesh, her flesh
gushed out over her corset, her stockings,
her tight white blouse collars.
He tired of saying goodbye.

She waited until Spring to die.
The crocuses were shining purple
in the morning and the neighbors
were venturing out in their cars.

That season after Grandma's death,
daily Grandpa put away the lunch fixings,
carefully saved his teabag
to be used again at dinner,
found a singular solace in going to the cemetery.
He knelt by the grave, stared at the marker –
her name, the epitaph "I'll walk slow", the years.

He remembered that he had once felt
his flesh on fire as she touched his thigh,
that they had curled their toes in the sand
at Crystal Beach and watched fireworks exploding,
that they had planned the blue cape cod
they would build in Fredonia,
the five children they would raise.

He pretended to feel no bitterness at being left
behind with the Blue Cross claim forms,
the box of Sarah Coventry earrings,
the remembering.

What I Tell Myself

After years of calling him, cleaning for him,
taking him to Friday lunches at Friendly's,
he is where I can't be.
The apartment is still full of his furniture.
I tell myself he's getting better.
I tell myself that isn't true.

The nursing home message says *he's*
fallen again, not hurt, no need to come in.
He calls and I praise him for remembering
the number, wanting to talk.
He tells me he has big, big problems---
his stalled car, dead battery. Will I go
to the blue garage on Peach Street
where they know how to charge it? I tell him
not to worry, I will take care of it.
He has no car, hasn't driven in five years.

I don't want to be where he's
gone, don't want to kneel next to his chair
and watch him pull an imaginary blanket
over his head, don't want to take his fingers out
of his mouth or wipe the saliva from his face.
I don't want to.

I remember the man who kept lists of every two dollar
contribution he made to the St. Jude's Children's Hospital,
the man who never left his apartment without his hat
or a lengthy look back to make sure the stove was off.
I want to believe this man doesn't see himself
as he is now, this man the nurses found
last night *naked with his call button*
wrapped around his neck.
Not hurt, no need to come in.

I tell myself he'll die soon.
I tell myself that isn't true.